POCKET BOOK OF
HOPE

First published in Great Britain 2020 by Trigger

Trigger is a trading style of Shaw Callaghan Ltd & Shaw Callaghan 23 USA, INC.

The Foundation Centre

Navigation House, 48 Millgate, Newark

Nottinghamshire NG24 4TS UK

www.triggerpublishing.com

British Library Cataloguing-in-Publication data

A CIP catalogue record for this book is available upon request
from the British Library

ISBN: 9781789561821

Cover design and typeset by Fusion Graphic Design Ltd.

Printed and bound in China by Hung Hing Printers Group Ltd.

Paper from responsible sources

POCKET BOOK OF

HOPE

www.triggerpublishing.com

INTRODUCTION

Modern life can be filled with so much: from the daily commute, a hectic schedule, cooking an evening meal; to those crucial turning points: quitting your job, moving house, finding love. Between the noise, it can be easy to lose hope, even when on the surface, things are going well.

The *Pocket Book of Hope* offers a little guidance for when the scales of life are tipped, times become turbulent and hope is in short supply. From the minds of some of the world's most well-known figures, learn to find your footing, take a breath and look to the future more positively.

The arc of the moral universe is long,
but it bends toward justice

Martin Luther King Jr.

Once you choose hope,
anything's possible

Christopher Reeve

Our greatest glory is not in never falling,
but in rising every time we fall

Confucius

May your choices reflect your hopes,
not your fears

Nelson Mandela

You must not lose faith in humanity.
Humanity is an ocean;
if a few drops of the ocean are dirty ...

... the ocean does not become dirty

Mahatma Gandhi

Hope is being able to see that there is light
despite all of the darkness

Desmond Tutu

In all things, it is better to hope
than to despair

Johann Wolfgang von Goethe

The best way to not feel hopeless is to get up and do something. Don't wait for good things to happen to you. If you go out and make some good things happen ...

... you will fill the world with hope,
you will fill yourself with hope

Barack Obama

Ever since happiness heard your name,
it has been running through the
streets trying to find you

Hafiz of Persia

Hope is passion for what is possible

Søren Kierkegaard

When things go wrong, don't go with them

Elvis Presley

I finally started to let that go
and embrace my own type of beauty.
Everyone's bodies are different,
and we all have different shapes ...

... but it has nothing to do with who you are

Camila Mendes

Youth is easily deceived
because it is quick to hope

Aristotle

When you're at the end of your rope,
tie a knot and hold on

Theodore Roosevelt

To live without hope
is to cease to live

Fyodor Dostoyevsky

This new day is too dear,
with its hopes and invitations, to waste
a moment on the yesterdays

Ralph Waldo Emerson

It's not the absence of fear,
it's overcoming it. Sometimes you've got
to blast through and have faith

Emma Watson

Many of life's failures are people
who did not realize how close they were to
success when they gave up

Thomas Edison

The miserable have no other medicine,
but only hope

William Shakespeare

Hope is that thing inside us that insists,
despite all the evidence to the contrary,
that something better awaits us if we
have the courage to reach for it ...

... and to work for it and to fight for it

Barack Obama

A leader is a dealer in hope

Napoleon Bonaparte

He who has a why to live
for can bear almost any how

Friedrich Nietzsche

Children are the world's most valuable
resource and its best hope for the future

John F. Kennedy

All things are difficult before they are easy

Thomas Fuller

Hope itself is like a star –
not to be seen in the sunshine of
prosperity, and only to be discovered
in the night of adversity

Charles Spurgeon

It is difficult to say what is impossible,
for the dream of yesterday is the hope of
today and the reality of tomorrow

Robert H. Goddard

If winter comes, can spring be far behind?

Percy Bysshe Shelley

To plant a garden is to believe in tomorrow

Audrey Hepburn

Through perseverance many people
win success out of what seemed
destined to be certain failure

Benjamin Disraeli

Hope is like the sun, which,
as we journey toward it, casts the shadow
of our burden behind us

Samuel Smiles

The great moral powers of
the soul are faith, hope, and love

Ellen G. White

Failure is a great teacher and,
if you are open to it, every mistake
has a lesson to offer

Oprah Winfrey

When the unthinkable happens,
the lighthouse is hope.

Christopher Reeve

Do not spoil what you have by
desiring what you have not;
remember that what you now
have was once among the
things you only hoped for

Epicurus

Don't judge each day by the
harvest you reap but by
the seeds that you plant

Robert Louis Stevenson

The future rewards those who press on.
I don't have time to feel sorry for myself.
I don't have time to complain.
I'm going to press on

Barack Obama

It's a good place when all you
have is hope and not expectations

Danny Boyle

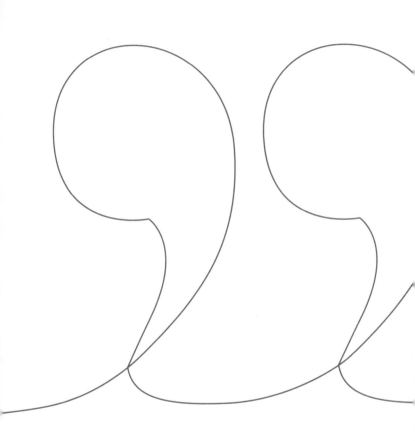

Forgiveness provides hope, joy, and
a bright future that nothing else can

Paul J. Meyer

Never give out while there is hope;
but hope not beyond reason, for that shows
more desire than judgment

William Penn

Out of difficulties grow miracles

Jean De La Bruyère

Hope is the dream of a waking man

Aristotle

Hope is the thing with feathers
that perches in the soul and sings the tunes
without the words and never stops at all

Emily Dickson

Such is hope, heaven's own gift
to struggling mortals, pervading, like
some subtle essence from the skies,
all things both good and bad

Charles Dickens

The natural flights of the human
mind are not from pleasure
to pleasure, but from hope to hope

Samuel Johnson

With high hope for the future,
no prediction is ventured

Abraham Lincoln

Hope is the struggle of the soul,
breaking loose from what is perishable,
and attesting her eternity

Herman Melville

Hope is nature's veil for
hiding truth's nakedness

Alfred Nobel

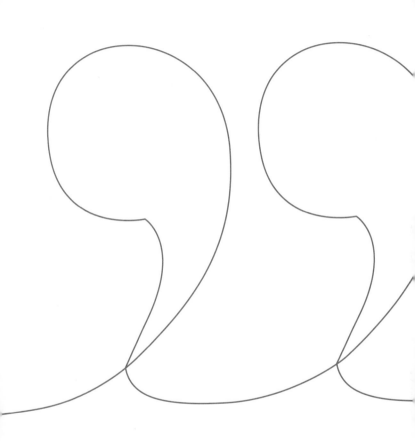

It is hope that gives life meaning.
And hope is based on the prospect of being
able one day to turn the actual world into a
possible one that looks better

François Jacob

Dream as if you'll live forever,
live as if you'll die today

James Dean

Perseverance is more prevailing
than violence; and many things which
cannot be overcome when they
are together, yield themselves up
when taken little by little

Plutarch

My hope still is to leave the world a
bit better than when I got here

Jim Henson

It's important for you to understand
that your experience facing and
overcoming adversity is actually one of
your biggest advantages

Michelle Obama

We are stronger in the places
we have been broken

Ernest Hemingway

There is no better than adversity.
Every defeat, every heartbreak, every loss,
contains its own seed, its own lesson on
how to improve your performance
the next time

Malcolm X

Start by doing what's necessary;
then do what's possible;
and suddenly you're doing
the impossible

Francis of Assisi

You can imprison a man, but not an idea.
You can exile a man, but not an idea.
You can kill a man, but not an idea

Benazir Bhutto

Let your hook be always cast.
In the pool where you least expect it,
will be fish

Ovid

What would the hero of your life's
movie do right now? Do that

Joe Rogan

Knowing what must be done
does away with fear

Rosa Parks

I hope the fathers and mothers of little girls
will look at them and say 'yes, women can'

Dilma Rousseff

Hopeful, we are halfway to where we
want to go; hopeless, we are lost forever

Lao Tzu

If you don't get out of the box
you've been raised in, you won't understand
how much bigger the world is

Angelina Jolie

Stop acting so small.
You are the universe in ecstatic motion

Rumi

Whenever you are blue or lonely or stricken by some humiliating thing you did, the cure and the hope is in caring about other people

Diane Sawyer

Faith has to do with things
that are not seen and hope
with things that are not at hand

Thomas Aquinas

Hope is sweet-minded and sweet-eyed.
It draws pictures; it weaves fancies;
it fills the future with delight

Henry Ward Beecher

You can never leave footprints
that last if you are always
walking on tiptoes

Leymah Gbowee

All human wisdom is summed
up in two words; wait and hope

Alexandre Dumas

Where there's life, there's hope

Theocritus

I learned compassion from
being discriminated against.
Everything bad that's ever
happened to me has
taught me compassion

Ellen DeGeneres

Courage is like love;
it must have hope for nourishment

Napoleon Bonaparte

If it were not for hopes,
the heart would break

Thomas Fuller

Hope smiles from the threshold
of the year to come,
whispering 'it will be happier'

Alfred Tennyson

What would happen if we
were all brave enough to be a
little bit more ambitious?
I think the world would change

Reese Witherspoon

My attitude is that if you push me towards something that you think is a weakness, then I will turn that perceived weakness into a strength

Michael Jordan

He who believes is strong;
he who doubts is weak.
Strong convictions precede
great actions

Louisa May Alcott

It does not matter how slowly you go,
as long as you do not stop

Confucius

To wish was to hope,
and to hope was to expect

Jane Austen

There is nothing like a dream
to create the future

Victor Hugo

Everything that is done in
this world is done by hope

Martin Luther

Even in the mud and scum of things,
something always, always sings

Ralph Waldo Emerson

Rules for happiness: something to do,
someone to love, something to hope for

Immanuel Kant

True hope is swift, and flies
with swallow's wings

William Shakespeare

In the midst of winter,
I find within me the invisible summer

Leo Tolstoy

We must pass through the darkness,
to reach the light

Albert Pike

You call it hope - that fire of fire!
It is but agony of desire

Edgar Allan Poe

Yes, evil often seems to surpass good.
But then, in spite of us, and without
our permission, there comes at last an
end to the bitter frosts. One morning
the wind turns, and there is a thaw.
And so I must still have hope

Vincent van Gogh

Just because you fail once doesn't mean
you're gonna fail at everything

Marilyn Monroe

I like the immaterial world.
I like to live among thoughts and
images of the past and the possible,
and even of the impossible,
now and then

Thomas Love Peacock

I thought that the light-house
looked lovely as hope, that star on
life's tremulous ocean

Thomas Moore

He who plants a tree, plants a hope

Lucy Larcom

Sometimes even to live is an act of courage

Seneca

So dry your tears. The storm has
not yet broken upon you with too
much violence. Your anchors are
holding firm ...

... and they permit you both comfort in the
present, and hope in the future

Boethius

Sometimes I can only groan,
and suffer, and pour out my
despair at the piano

Frédéric Chopin

The greater the obstacle,
the more glory in overcoming it

Molière

The most common form of despair
is not being who you are

Søren Kierkegaard

I am a slow walker,
but I never walk back

Abraham Lincoln

But what we call our despair
is often only the painful
eagerness of unfed hope

George Eliot

A wise man will make more opportunities than he finds

Francis Bacon

Perseverance is failing 19 times
and succeeding the 20th

Julie Andrews

The man who moves a mountain begins
by carrying away small stones

Confucius

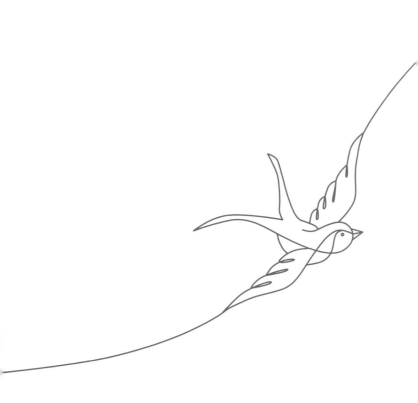

Courage is not having
the strength to go on;
it is going on when you
don't have the strength

Theodore Roosevelt

Let me tell you the secret
that has led to my goal.
My strength lies solely in my tenacity

Louis Pasteur

I was taught the way of
progress is neither swift nor easy

Marie Curie

Patience is the art of hoping

Luc De Clapiers

Keep the faith, don't lose
your perseverance and always
trust your gut instinct

Paula Abdul

The most glorious moments in your life
are not the so-called days of success,
but rather those days when out of
dejection and despair ...

... you feel rise in you a challenge to life

Gustave Flaubert

It's perseverance that's the key.
It's persevering for long enough
to achieve your potential

Lynn Davies

Every strike brings me closer
to the next home run

Babe Ruth

Education is the passport to the future,
for tomorrow belongs to those who
prepare for it today

Malcolm X

The best way to predict the future
is to create it

Abraham Lincoln

Make the most of moments that matter

Kate Middleton, Duchess of Cambridge

Hope in the face of difficulty. Hope in
the face of uncertainty. The audacity of hope!
In the end, that is God's greatest gift
to us, the bedrock of this nation. A belief in
things not seen. A belief that there are
better days ahead

Barack Obama

I hope I can be as good of a father to my son as my dad was to me

Calvin Johnson

Hope is patience with the lamp lit

Tertullian

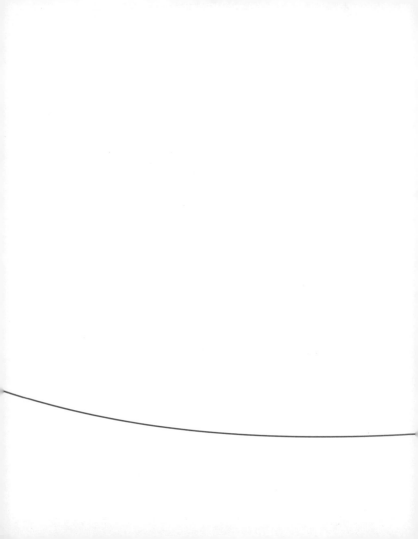

For a little guidance elsewhere ...

POCKET BOOK OF

FRIENDSHIP

For when life gets a little tough

POCKET BOOK OF

HAPPINESS

For when life gets a little tough

TRIGGER™
The mental health & wellbeing publisher

www.triggerpublishing.com

We want to help you to not just survive
but thrive ... one book at a time

Find out more about Trigger Publishing by visiting our website:
triggerpublishing.com or join us on:

@TriggerPub

the *Shaw* mind
FOUNDATION

A proportion of profits from the sale of all Trigger
books go to their sister charity, The Shaw Mind Foundation,
founded by Adam Shaw and Lauren Callaghan.

The charity aims to ensure that everyone has access
to mental health resources whenever they need them.

Find out more: **shawmindfoundation.org** or join them on:

@Shaw_Mind   @ShawMindFoundation   @Shaw_Mind